THE OFFICIAL
RONALD WILSON REAGAN
Quote Book

Chain-Pinkham Books

Chain-Pinkham Books
6414 Cambridge Street
St. Louis Park,
Minnesota 55426

Copyright © 1980 by Chain-Pinkham Books
Library of Congress Catalog No.: 80-70790
ISBN: 0-938948-00-8

First Printing, December, 1980

Printed in the U.S.A.

TABLE OF CONTENTS

Camelot is not dead.
Camelot is this country
and Camelot will die only
if we we fail to meet
our responsibilities
and keep our principles alive
for the world.

Speech at New Orleans, 10/26/68

A little while ago
they were calling out Bonzo.
They'd better be careful.
Bonzo grew up to be King Kong.

Battlecreek, Mich., 11/1/80

A wind is blowing across
this state of ours.
And it is not only wind;
it will grow into a tidal wave.
And there will be a
government with men as tall
as mountains.

Campaign, 1966

Campaign '80

DEBATE BUTTERFLIES? — I've been on the same stage with John Wayne.

Time, 11/10/80

Depression is when you're out of work. A recession is when your neighbor's out of work. Recovery is when Carter's out of work.

Time, 9/8/80

I haven't had Jimmy Carter's experience. I wouldn't be caught dead with it.

Hell, I could have campaigned on the same things he campaigned on. The only difference was he forgot them between Plains and Washington.

Time, 6/30/80

CARTER — In California, I kept trying to do the things I said I was going to do. He had a record and, damn it, he was not a good Governor.

Time, 6/30/80

THE DEBATE — It seemed to go all right. I've examined myself and I can't find any wounds.

IN THE SOUTH BRONX — What I'm trying to tell you is I can't do a damn thing for you if I'm not elected.

Time, 8/18/80

President ,

I never had any great hunger for the job, the title or living in that house. But there were things I believed in that I thought I could do and certainly for that reason there is disappointment.

San Francisco Chronicle, 9/2/76

HIS SACRAMENTO MANSION — I'm not one to look a gift house in the mouth.

2/3/67

Gosh, it's taken me all my life to get up the nerve to do what I'm doing. . . that's as far as my dreams go.

1966

Well, you know, a headshrinker, he's probably sitting there looking at the pupils in my eyes on television. He can see me on a couch now. Well, I want to tell you, if I get on that couch, it will be to take a nap.

Every once in a while I pinch myself sitting opposite a head of state of one or another of a dozen nations we've visited, thinking this can't be 'Dutch' Reagan here. I should still be out on the dock at Lowell Park.

The basic freedoms: the freedom to worship, the freedom to choose your occupation, the freedom to try and fail and, if need be, to try again, the freedom to make mistakes and to do things others might consider stupid.

Call to Action, 1976

The voice from that podium is louder than any voice out there in the countryside.

One thing our Founding Fathers could not foresee – they were farmers, professional men, businessmen giving of their time and effort to an idea that became a country – was a nation governed by professional politicians who had a vested interest in getting re-elected. They probably envisioned a fellow serving a couple of hitches and then looking eagerly forward to getting back to the farm.

Speech to students, 1973

Patriot

Call it mysticism if you will, I have always believed that there was some divine plan that placed this nation between the oceans to be sought out and found by those with a special kind of courage and an overabundant love of freedom.

Speech, 7/4/68

BIRTH AND INFANCY — My face was blue from screaming, my bottom was red from whacking, and my father claimed afterward he was white when he said shakily, "For such a little bit of a fat Dutchman, he makes a hell of a lot of noise, doesn't he?"
Ever since my birth my nickname has been "Dutch" and I have been particularly fond of the colors that were exhibited – red, white, and blue. I have not been uncomfortable on the various occasions when I have had an overwhelming impulse to brandish them.

Where's the Rest of Me?, 1965

The Constitution was never conceived as a shield for degeneracy. You start out burning the flag and you end up burning Detroit.

Ronnie & Jesse, 1969

If indeed America does have aggressive designs on the world, then how do we explain those days after World War II when the United States had the greatest military strength in history and a monopoly on the nuclear bomb – why didn't America impose its will on the world?

YAF Convention, Anaheim, CA., 4/23/71

Not too long ago two friends of mine were talking to a Cuban refugee. He was a business man who had escaped from Castro. In the midst of his tale of horrible experiences, one of my friends turned to the other and said, "We don't know how lucky we are." The Cuban stopped and said, "How lucky you are? *I* had some place to escape to."

TV Address, 10/27/64

Our Constitution is a document that protects the people from government.

Reagan: The Political Chameleon, 1976

The people's instincts are still right. You see them come to the rescue of someone – a child who falls down a well – hundreds of people rush to help, and labor and equipment are volunteered without any thought of who's going to pay for it. This is a basic feeling in Americans. They don't stand back in such a circumstance and ask what government's going to do about it.

Call to Action, 1976

LINCOLN'S AND WASHINGTON'S BIRTHDAYS — In an attempt to achieve the maximum work-load output for the dollar spent by the state, we are requesting that all state employees voluntarily come to work on Monday, Feb. 13, and on Feb. 22.

Memo to Employees, 2/7/67

...and Politician

There seems to be something blarney-green in the blood of most Sons of the Old Sod – as proved by the recent political history of the country – that gives zest to the shillelagh psyche. I had been lauded as a star in sports and had been praised in movies: in politics I found myself misrepresented, cursed, vilified, denounced, and libeled. Yet it was by far the most fascinating part of my life.

Where's the Rest of Me?, 1965

JOHN BIRCH — I don't believe I have any moral justification for repudiating them.

What Makes Reagan Run?, 1968

These employees I was meeting were a cross-section of America and, damn it, too many of our political leaders, our labor leaders, and certainly a lot of geniuses in my own business and on Madison Avenue have underestimated them. They want the truth, they are friendly and helpful, intelligent and alert.

Where's the Rest of Me?, 1965

I think one of the most dangerous slogans ever coined is "the greatest good for the greatest number." A noble-sounding phrase, but what does it really mean? It means that 50% of the people plus one can do whatever they want to the rest, by rationalizing that what they're doing to them is "good."

I was out on location in the country when I was called to the telephone at an oil station. I was told that if I made the report a squad was ready to take care of me and fix my face so I would never be in pictures again.

Testimony at 1954 Court Hearing

One plant distributed over ten thousand photos, and in two days I signed all of them. It's the only time I ever blistered a finger just writing. In another town they had a reception and I stood in a receiving line and shook two thousand hands. After the first one thousand it seemed that everyone not only had an iron grip but managed to land their thumbs on the exact same spot. no matter how I twisted or turned my hand. It became the sheer agony of a bone bruise. At Appliance Park in Louisville, Kentucky, there were forty-six miles of assembly line – I walked all of them, twice. I had to meet the night shift too.

Where's the Rest of Me?, 1965

In 1938, a novice in Hollywood, I suddenly found myself on the board of the SAG. One of the vacancies happened to fit my classification: new, young contract player. I accepted with awe and pleasure. My education was completed when I walked into the board room. I saw it crammed with the famous men of the business. I knew then I was beginning to find the rest of me.

Where's the Rest of Me?, 1965

Professional politicians like to talk about the value of experience in government. Nuts! The only experience you gain in politics is how to be political.

Call to Action, 1976

There's an old legend about the politician who looks out his window and sees his constituents marching by. "There go my people," he says. "I must hasten to find out where they're going so I can get in front and lead them."

I am speaking here today neither as an academician nor as a politician. I do not have the training to be the first nor the aspiration to be the second.

Kansas State University, 10/26/67

Himself

I have heard more than one psychiatrist say that we imbibe our ideals from our mother's milk. Then, I must say, my breast feeding was the home of the brave baby and the free bosom. I was the hungriest person in the house but I only got chubby when I exercised in the crib; any time I wasn't gnawing on the bars, I was worrying with my thumb in my mouth – habits which have symbolically persisted throughout my life.

Where's the Rest of Me?, 1965

Our family didn't exactly come from the wrong side of the tracks, but we were certainly always within sound of the train whistles... my father never made more than fifty-five dollars *a week* in his whole life.

Where's the Rest of Me?, 1965

I was born in a small town in the Midwest, and I was in poverty before the rich folks got hold of it.

Where's the Rest of Me?, 1965

CARVING TURKEY — This was something I had to learn after I grew up, because when I was a kid we couldn't afford a turkey.

11/14/73

I loved three things: drama, politics, and sports, and I'm not sure they always come in that order.

Where's the Rest of Me?, 1965

I'm a lazy fellow. I work up to a certain point, but beyond that point, I say the hell with it.

LIFEGUARD — I got to recognize that people hate to be saved: almost every one of them later sought me out and angrily denounced me for dragging them to shore. "I would have been fine if you'd let me alone," was their theme. "You made a fool out of me trying to make a hero out of yourself."

Where's the Rest of Me?, 1965

Out in the fields, I disliked beating snakes to death because they seemed to suffer but I got a wild exhiliration out of jumping feet first into a pile-up. We used the immemorial rules that are standard for any gang of boys on their own.

Where's the Rest of Me?, 1965

I love desserts, so I'm lucky with a metabolism that burns up pretty much everything.

All I do for my hair is bake it in the sun, boil it under the shower, comb with water and use a little dab of Brylcreem to hold it down.

4/1/74

There is no foundation to the rumor that I am the only one here who was at the original Al Smith dinner.

35th Annual Al Smith Dinner, New York

I'm not smart enough to lie.

Time, 10/20/80

Maybe there is nothing wrong with a little maturity — someone who remembers the Great Depression.

San Diego, 1979

I don't want to go back to the so-called simple life. It wasn't simple at all.

Time, 10/20/80

FATHER — Jack (we all called him by his nickname) was a handsome man – tall, swarthy, and muscular, filled with contradictions of character. A sentimental Democrat, who believed fervently in the rights of the workingman – I recall him cursing vehemently about the battle at Herrin in 1922, where twenty-six persons were killed in a massacre brought about by a coal-mine strike – he never lost his conviction that the individual must stand on his own feet. Once he caught me fighting in the schoolyard, surrounded by a circle of eggers-on. He stopped the fight, tongue-lashed the crowd – then lifted me a foot in the air with the flat side of his boot. "Not because you were fighting," he said, "but because you weren't winning."

Where's the Rest of Me?, 1965

Democrats & Republicans

I have spent most of my life as a Democrat. I recently have seen fit to follow another course. I believe that the issues confronting us cross party lines. I have an uncomfortable feeling that this prosperity isn't something upon which we can base our hopes for the future.

TV Address, 1964

CALIFORNIA'S 11TH COMMANDMENT — Thou shalt not speak ill of any other Republican.

I sometimes wonder what the Ten Commandments would have looked like if Moses had to run them through a Democratic Legislature.

Ronnie & Jesse, 1969

I've never been able to understand how the Democrats can run those $1,000-a-plate dinners at such a profit, and run the Government at such a loss.

Dallas, 10/26/67

I didn't desert my party. It deserted me. I looked up FDR's old platform, and I discovered that it called for a restoration of states' rights and a reduction in the national budget. You know what? I'm still for that.

I think people have been pretty wonderful, other than those looking for something to criticize.

5/11/67

War & Peace

RUSSIA — They are bent on world conquest, and what we're bent on is a strategy of deterring them from advancing their cause by gunfire.

San Francisco Chronicle, 7/7/77

NUCLEAR BOMBS — No one, of course, wants to use these weapons but the enemy should never be told we won't. He should go to bed every night fearful that we might.

1966

I do not want to live in a world where the Soviet Union is Number One.

I guess the biggest reaction of anything I say is to my line that maybe we should stop worrying about whether the rest of the world likes us, and decide we are going to be respected in the world as we once were.

Time, 11/26/79

No more abandonments of friends by the U.S. We don't care if we're not liked. We're going to be respected.

Columbus, GA., 1980

But when has deciding to settle for a draw ever kept a bully from starting another fight?

The U.S is in a more precarious position today than it was the day after Pearl Harbor.

Time, 11/26/79

We dare not allow America to become weak and defenseless because if we do, the day could come when we would not be divided into hawks or doves – just pigeons.

YAF Convention, Anaheim, CA., 4/23/71

We know that Russia has quadrupled its espionage and counterintelligence activities related to the United States in just the last couple of years. Yet our own intelligence sources all over the world are drying up because they fear that inevitable leaks from Congressional investigations of the CIA will cost them their lives.

Call to Action, 1976

We've been very successful in fighting wars, when we had to, with civilian control and with citizen soldiers serving only temporarily in the military. The attitude of the American army has always been: "Let's get this thing over with so we can go home and do what we want to." We haven't been militarily bookbound. In World War I the European generals knew what their opponents would do because they all had read the same books. They weren't prepared for a bunch of Americans whose logic was simply, "Where are they and how do we get at them?"

Call to Action, 1976

It is cheap demagoguery to suggest that anyone would want to send other people's sons to war. The only argument is with regard to the best way to avoid war. There is only one sure way – surrender.

TV Address, 10/27/64

RECLASSIFYING DRAFT DODGERS — Emotionally I could go along with him. . . intellectually I realize we can't make military service punitive.

Yale, 1967

ON VIETNAM — We should declare war on North Vietnam. We could pave the whole place over by noon and be home for dinner.

When 50,000 Americans make the ultimate sacrifice to defend the people of a small, defenseless country in Southeast Asia from Communist tyranny, that, my friends, is a collective act of moral courage, not an example of moral poverty.

Time, 2/11/80

I'm not trigger happy. There have been four wars in my lifetime. . . none came about because the U.S. was too strong.

Time, 6/30/80

It would be a mistake to tell the enemy we would never use nuclear weapons. I don't believe in a war where the other side has a kind of feeling they have a sanctuary, and we have none.

Countdown '68, 1967

I have wondered why we couldn't evolve a program of inducement to enlistment, incentives to enlist, to see if we could not switch to a voluntary system. . . I am fearful of long-time compulsory military service becoming what it was in years past in Europe, where the uniform becomes a matter of servitude, and not of patriotism.

Countdown '68, 1967

In due time I became a captain but, when I was proposed for major, I asked that the recommendation be canceled. I know the fortunes of war are distributed unevenly, but who was I to be a major for serving in California, without ever hearing a shot fired in anger?

Where's the Rest of Me?, 1965

Colonel Ferguson turned me over to the adjutant at Fort Mason on that first day of my military service. I discovered that, even though I was in, another physical was required. I went through the same old business with the eyes, and one of the two examining doctors said, "If we sent you overseas, you'd shoot a general."

The other doctor looked up and said, "Yes, and you'd miss him."

Where's the Rest of Me?, 1965

Their signs said make love, not war, but they didn't look like they could do either.

Ronnie & Jesse, 1969

Foreign Affairs

Punting from behind one's own goal posts is one of the most dangerous plays in football. We are trying to do the same thing in our international life and, at the same time, pretend that it is a winning touchdown play. It may be. But smart gamblers will give long odds that you will lose.

Where's the Rest of Me?, 1965

Watergate was a disaster to our foreign policy. Richard Nixon had taken us a long way toward a realistic plan for strategic balance with the communists. He was coldly realistic about the Russians. He could meet and confer with them, drink toasts with them. But, unlike the previous leaders we had sent over there, who thought every time the communists smiled they had quit being communists, Nixon never forgot that they were really intent on world domination.

Call to Action, 1976

I know that a large part of dealing in foreign affairs is just the same type of common sense that I found was necessary when, as the president of my union, I sat across the table and to bargain with management and not blow my cool or give in too soon.

Reagan: The Political Chameleon, 1976

There's no question that the self-sufficiency and material well-being of Americans are being diminished by government. We're following England down the road to intellectual and financial destruction.

Call to Action, 1976

Government

My idea of the way to start is to take Government off the backs of the people and make you free again!

Time, 10/20/80

Already the hour is late, government has laid its hand on health, housing, farming, industry, commerce, education, and to an ever increasing degree interferes with the people's right to know.

I've heard drug experts say that they believe penicillin, if it were discovered today, would not be licensed by the FDA.

I used to fantasize what it would be like if everyone in Government would quietly slip away and close the doors and disappear. See how long it would take the people of this country to miss them. I think that life would go on, and the people would keep right on doing the things they are doing, and we would get along a lot better than we think.

Time, 11/26/79

If you look back you find that those great social reforms really didn't work. They didn't cure unemployment. They didn't solve social problems. What came from them was a group of people who became entrenched in Government, who wanted social reforms just for the sake of social reforms.

Time, 7/21/80

And this, I believe, is what the political contest has been all about in recent years. Are we going to have an elitist Government that makes the decisions for people's lives, or are we going to believe, as we had for so many decades, that the people can make these decisions themselves?

Time, 10/20/80

If I appointed him, he's qualified.

I ran for governor without experience. Sometimes it helps – you don't know what you can't do.

It never occurred to me to give a saliva test to the people that have supported me.

Today, if you don't like the laws in your state you can move. When the federal government takes control, there is no place to move to.

Call to Action, 1976

We simply have to cut government off at the pockets.

Call to Action, 1976

I have an opponent who says money is the mother's milk of politics, and you've never seen a baby who has so much squawk about where the milk comes from.

Ronnie & Jesse, 1969

Congress will bow to the will of the people, just as the California Legislature did. You don't have to convert Congress – save their souls – you just have to make them feel the heat.

Call to Action, 1976

To complete the reforms we needed changes in the state laws, and of course the legislature just laughed at us. So we took our case to the people, and pretty soon the people began to let their legislators know that they wanted action. The flood of telegrams, cards, and letters was so great that finally the speaker of the California Assembly came into my office with his hands up. He surrendered, and we got the new law we needed.

Call to Action, 1976

Government, when it is bent at all, is bent to the wills of special interest groups, whose goals are always in opposition to the general interest. The great mass of people has been too busy working to pay the bills and the taxes; they're not organized. They only get a chance to make their will known at election time.

Call to Action, 1976

FIRST 100 DAYS — I had been led to believe there was a honeymoon period but evidently I lost the license on the way to the church because I haven't had any honeymoon for a hundred days.

4/4/67

You and I can start a prairie fire that will sweep across the country and restore to government a full measure of confidence.

Gubernatorial Campaign, 1966

If someone supports me, that means he accepts my philosophy. I haven't bought his.

Countdown '68

Government is like a baby – an alimentary canal with an appetite at one end and no sense of responsibility at the other.

The credibility gap is so great in Washington they told us the truth the other day hoping we wouldn't believe it.

Ronnie & Jesse, 1969

Once in a while when you come to a tough problem, you choose someone who doesn't know anything about it because he doesn't know what you can't do.

Where's the Rest of Me?, 1965

The fact that anyone at any time can move across a state line is a protection against tyranny in state government.

Sincerely, Ronald Reagan, 1967

As far as I'm concerned, California has no finer representatives or better ambassadors than the Rams.

Letter to George Allen

...and Bureaucracy

Our problem isn't a shortage of fuel, it's a surplus of government.

San Francisco, 1/18/78

Because no government ever voluntarily reduces itself in size, government programs once launched never go out of existence. A government agency is the nearest thing to eternal life we'll ever see on this earth.

TV Address. 10/27/64

This man sits at a desk in Washington. Documents come to him each morning. He reads them, initials them, and passes them on to the proper agency. One day a document arrived he wasn't supposed to read, but he read it, initialed it and passed it on. Twenty-four hours later it arrived back at his desk with a memo attached that said, "You weren't supposed to read this. Erase your initials and initial the erasure."

I've got a farm. Now you get a 19-page questionaire – you're expected to answer how many acres are in crops, how many acres are in timberland or pasture. I just threw the damn thing in the wastebasket the last few years and I haven't gotten any follow-up at all. They've stopped sending the forms.

Time, 6/30/80

No matter how much the bureaucrats deny it, the purse strings always end up manipulating the policy.

Call to Action, 1976

Bureaucracy does not take kindly to being assailed and isn't above using a few low blows and a knee to the groin when it fights back. Knowing this, I have become extremely cautious in dealing with government agencies.

Where's the Rest of Me?, 1965

You know they have 144 rules for climbing a ladder.

San Francisco, 1978

We have been told that the problems are too complex for simple answers, until gradually we have accepted government by mystery; there seems to have evolved a special kind of government language, incomprehensible to simple citizens like ourselves.

Where's the Rest of Me?, 1965

Taxes

The entire graduated income tax structure was created by Karl Marx. It has no justification in getting the government needed revenue.

What Makes Reagan Run?, 1968

Why should we be taking social security taxes from the pay of a teenager working part-time?   Why, other than to feed government's greed?   It certainly has nothing to do with the teenager's welfare.

But there are the privileged few who don't have to pay those taxes and don't have to worry about the effects of potential Social Security bankruptcy on their retirement incomes. The civilian employees of the federal government –some 3 million of them – have lobbied feverishly for 40 years to keep themselves out of Social Security. Now that it's in trouble they have nothing to lose. All these years they've been betting *our* money on a sure loser, at no risk to themselves.

I hope there's nothing Freudian in the fact that I ran into difficulty when I started talking about taxes on liquor and insurance.

Speech to State Legislature, 1967

True, I'd been making handsome money ever since World War II, but that handsome money lost a lot of its beauty and substance going through the 91 percent bracket of the income tax. The tragic fact of life in this evil day of progressive taxation is that, once behind, it is well-nigh impossible to earn your way out.

Where's the Rest of Me?, 1965

Why is it inflationary to let the people keep more of their money and spend it the way they'd like, and it isn't inflationary to let (the President) take that money and spend it the way he wants?

Time, 11/10/80

Humor

"How do you tell the Polish one at a cockfight?"
"He's the one with the duck."
"How do you tell the Italian?"
"He bet on the duck."
"How do you know the Mafia is there?"
"The duck wins."

From now on, I'm going to look over both shoulders, and then I'm only going to tell stories about Irishmen, because I'm Irish.

DEVELOPING AFRICAN NATIONS — When they have a man for lunch, they *really* have him for lunch.

What Makes Reagan Run?, 1968

HIS NEW HOME — It'll have everything electric except a chair.

Las Vegas is really a wonderful place. Where else outside of government do people throw money away?

Keeping up with Governor Brown's promises is like reading Playboy magazine while your wife turns the pages.

Campaign Speech

Bobby Kennedy is making Lyndon Johnson so nervous he's thinking of putting the country in his wife's name.

BLAMED FOR ILLEGITIMATE BIRTH RISE — Thanks very much for sending me the clipping. I have never felt quite so young and virile. *Sincerely, Ronald Reagan, 1967*

Labor

UNEMPLOYMENT INSURANCE — It provides prepaid vacations for a segment of our society which has made it a way of life.

What Makes Reagan Run?, 1968

There are also a lot of jobs available that some people now call "menial." Maybe we need to get back the Depression mentality, where there were no menial jobs. A job was a job, and anyone who got one felt lucky.

Call to Action, 1976

I believe the biggest threat is big government, but it is supported by and feeds on big labor, and I fear that there are those in business who see a chance at monopoly, whether they use the word or not, if they go along with big government. I'm afraid the fight is never-ending, but we must continue.

My suggestion therefore is that you persuade the agriculture industry of your state to invite Cesar Chavez to come and organize the farm workers of Pennsylvania. This is a sacrifice California is prepared to make in the interest of human compassion.

Letter to Gov. Milton Shapp of Pennsylvania

When George Meany testifies to Congress that this country can afford a $100 billion deficit to solve the unemployment problem, it's obvious that he's been the victim of bad advice. If we overspend by $100 billion now, he'll be back asking that we overspend by $250 billion the next time. When government uses a deficit to create work, it also creates inflation.

Call to Action, 1976

UNIONS DECRYING USE OF STATE PRISONERS TO HARVEST CROPS — Sometimes they remind me of, you know, a dog sitting on a sharp rock howling with pain (that) is too stupid to get up.

Reagan: The Political Chameleon, 1976

...and Business

The system has never failed us once. But we have failed the system every time we lose faith in the magic of the market place.

San Francisco, 1/19/78

My first summer job, when I was 14 years old, was for an outfit that bought up old houses and remodeled them. I started in digging foundations and hauling away debris, but before the summer was over I had laid hardwood floor, painted houses — everything that had to be done to remodel a place. At the end of each week the boss reached in his pocket and paid me in cash. He didn't have to keep records of my hours, pay withholding and Social Security taxes for me, or provide workmen's compensation, health and life insurance, coffee breaks, and sterilized paper towels. The only person he had to pay for my labor was me, and that made me worth it to him.

I know I should be impressed about Edison inventing the lightbulb, but Edison himself would be impressed by the machine that spins those bulbs out like peas from a pod.

Where's the Rest of Me?, 1965

RETURN TO THE GOLD STANDARD? — I know it would be complicated to go back to a gold standard as such, but I am looking at a de facto gold standard. Suppose the U.S. set a date and said we are going to mint a coin based on the value of gold at that time. Once people realized they could take paper dollars and buy a gold coin of the same face value, they probably wouldn't bother to, and it would stabilize the value of the dollar.

Business Week, 3/31/80

But the truth is that outside of its legitimate function, government does nothing as well or as economically as the private sector of the economy.

TV Address, 10/27/64

I've always been opposed to monopoly, always believed that monopoly is evil. I don't care whether it's corporate monopoly, or government monopoly, or labor monopoly, it's monopoly thats evil, not who's doing it.

Call to Action, 1976

The greatest technological revolution in world history hasn't really been in space or any of the other exotic industries, but in American farming.

Sincerely, Ronald Reagan, 1967

Education

EUGENE MCCARTHY ENDORSEMENT — Maybe this will give some people confidence that I don't eat my young.

Time 11/3/80

I'm sick at what has happened at Berkeley. Sick of the sit-ins, the teach-ins, the walkouts. When I am elected Governor, I will organize a throw-out.

1965

There has been a leadership gap and a morality and decency gap at the University of California at Berkeley where a small minority of beatniks, radicals and filthy speech advocates have brought such shame to and such a loss of confidence in a great university.

San Francisco, 5/12/66

I was so busy with these other things that I apportioned only a certain amount of time to study. A C average was required for eligibility for outside activities. I set my goals at maintaining eligibility. I know that wasn't right but it also made room and time for other things that I think were valuable.

The Rise of Ronald Reagan, 1968

What good is it to teach someone all the facts if they don't know how to live and if they don't know the use of them for the solutions of the problems they are going to meet as life goes on.

Will we meet (the students') neurotic vulgarities with vacillation and weakness, or will we tell those entrusted with administering the university we expect them to enforce a code based on decency, common sense and dedication to the high and noble purpose of the University?

1/4/66

STUDENT PROTESTS — If there is to be a bloodbath, let it be now.

Congressional Quarterly, 1976

HISTORY PROFESSORS — According to them, it is the United States that has aggressive ambitions which cause the Soviets to arm defensively for protection. Logic obviously is not part of the approved course for at least some history teachers.

YAF Convention, Anaheim, CA., 4/23/71

STUDENT DEMONSTRATORS — I'd like to harness their youthful energy with a strap.

What Makes Reagan Run?, 1968

Preservation of free speech does not justify letting beatniks and advocates of sexual orgies, drug usage, and 'filthy speech' disrupt the academic community and interfere with our universities' purpose.

Countdown '68, 1967

Free tuition is not a right; it is a privilege of the deserving.

TV Address, 10/27/64

I oppose federal aid to education because no one has been able to prove the need for it.

What Makes Reagan Run?, 1968

Welfare

The men who first settled here (in Columbia, California) 118 years ago were a pretty colorful lot. They came west without an OEO grant. They camped and lived without benefit of the Area Development Agency making room, or the Rural Electrification Administration supplying the comforts. They and their new neighbors did not wait for Aid to Dependent Children. They looked after their own. Their children built great cities, an incredible railway and a series of magnificent valley farms. They played a small part in the greatest war on poverty this nation has ever seen.

Columbia, CA., 7/4/68

You are actually being taxed to provide better medical care for these card holders than you can afford for yourself or your family.

TV Address, 1967

I realize now, looking back on it, that we were poor, but I didn't know it at the time. I think this is one thing that might be wrong today. The government seems intent on telling people they are poor. One of the reasons we didn't know it was that my mother was always finding someone who needed help.

The Rise of Ronald Reagan, 1968

I'm sure everyone feels sorry for the individual who has fallen by the wayside or who can't keep up in our competitive society, but my own compassion goes beyond that to those millions of unsung men and women who get up every morning, send the kids to school, go to work, try to keep up the payments on their house, pay exorbitant taxes to make possible compassion for the less fortunate, and as a result have to sacrifice many of their own desires and dreams and hopes. Government owes them something better than always finding a new way to make them share the fruit of their toils with others.

Sincerely, Ronald Reagan, 1967

A man may choose to sit and fish instead of working – that's his pursuit of happiness. He does not have the right to force his neighbors to support him.

Sincerely, Ronald Reagan, 1967

GOVERNOR PAT BROWN — Well, he's good to his family . . . he's put a lot of relatives on the payroll.

1966 Gubernatorial Campaign

You can vote with your feet in this country. If a state is mismanaged you can move elsewhere.

The time has come for us to stop being our brother's keeper and become our brother's brother.

1967

FOOD STAMP PROGRAM — A multi-million dollar administrative nightmare, a staggering financial burden at the federal level and the newest nesting place for the welfare abuse and fraud.

8/11/74

Food stamps have become a massive subsidy for some of the exotic experiments in group living you have read about, what the sociologists call the underground culture.

The MediCal patient has a credit card. It is unlimited.

The elimination of poverty was a worthy goal in itself but during the Depression we had an all-time low in crime. I cannot help but believe that goods and privileges carelessly given or lightly earned are lightly regarded.

The state is a great fictitious entity by which everybody expects to live at the expense of everyone else. What price are we willing to pay for material security?

With Medicaid you've got a free credit card. The first little quiver of pain he says, "I'm going to the doctor." We found that the Medicaid patients spend an average of five times as long in the hospital as the private patient does for the same operation or illness. You and I in the hospital, we're figuring costs. We begin to say to the doctor, "When can I go home?" But they've never had a servant. They are lying there being waited on.

Politics Today, 1980

I believe the time has come for a new noblesse oblige by the American aristocracy of accomplishment.

Sincerely, Ronald Reagan, 1967

Environment

Environmental extremists wouldn't let you build a house unless it looked like a bird's nest.

Newsweek, 11/3/80

A tree is a tree – how many more do you need to look at.

Western Wood Products Association, 9/12/65

California is proud to be the home of the freeway.

11/13/73

There is no shortage of the energy with which we run the government of California, which we run on jelly beans!

4/26/74

One Saturday afternoon, during the campaign to decide whether or not there should be a Coastal Commission, I took a helicopter ride from Los Angeles to San Diego. We passed several state beaches, some crowded and some virtually empty. They had the same facilities, and in some cases the crowded beach and the empty beach were within a quarter-mile of each other. Obviously many beach-goers prefer to be crowded together. Buying more beaches that people won't go to because they prefer to be crowded together on one beach is a ridiculous waste of our natural resources and our taxes.

Call to Action, 1976

A strange sort of no-growth, no-development syndrome is proposed without regard for the consequences this might have on the lives of our people or the vitality of our economy. It is time to remember that we are ecology too.

Last year Germany conducted an experiment to determine the effects of leaded and unleaded gasoline. They pumped leaded exhaust fumes into one greenhouse and unleaded into another. Plants in both greenhouses were damaged, but when the exhaust fumes were turned off, the plants recovered faster in the greenhouse that had been pumped full of leaded fumes. What's more, not a trace of lead was found in the new vegetation after recovery.

Call to Action, 1976

Hysterical pollution leads to political pollution with the result that all too often little or nothing gets done about actual pollution. Let me give you some examples of hysterical pollution. A letter arrives on my desk signed by an entire schoolroom of eight-year-olds. They beg me to save them from smothering to death before they can grow up. Obviously they had been frightened into mailing such a letter by some adult who should know better. Another letter, again from school children, expresses a belief that very soon all the redwood trees will have been cut down and replaced by plastic imitations.

Letter to Steve Hansch, 1967

People seem to think that all redwoods that are not protected through a national park will disappear. I'll be damned if I take away all this privately owned land for no reason.

Minutes of Cabinet Meeting, 1967

Fun & Games

One of our good friends is Carroll Righter, who has a syndicated column on astrology. Every morning Nancy and I turn to see what he has to say about people of our respective birth signs.

Where's the Rest of Me?, 1965

Everything is a game except football. It is the last thing in our civilized life where a man can physically throw himself, his full body, into combat with another man.

Where's the Rest of Me?, 1965

My eyes were my big handicap in sports. I never cared for baseball, for example, because I was ball-shy at batting. When I stood at the plate, the ball appeared out of nowhere about two feet in front if me. I was always the last chosen for a side in any game. Then I discovered football: no little invisible ball – just another guy to grab or knock down, and it didn't matter if his face was blurred. I sat in the front row at school and still could not read the blackboard; I bluffed my lessons and got fairly good marks, considering.

Where's the Rest of Me?, 1965

I think I have to stick to horseback riding. You see, there is the matter of security. When I go any place, I'm one of a group. We might look like Hell's Angels with all of us out there on motorcycles.

Sincerely, Ronald Reagan, 1967

Conservatives

Some of you may remember that in my early years I was sort of a bleeding heart liberal. Then I became a man and put away childish ways.

Chico State College, 10/3/68

The right wing has a bad image. It's funny, people think of them as obstreperous and objectionable. But I don't see them at lie-ins, or teach-ins at the White House.

What Makes Reagan Run?, 1968

The so-called conservative today is someone who wants less Government power, less centralization of authority, more individual freedom. That was once called "liberal."

U.S. News, 8/29/77

There are those who will say having me here as speaker is a perfect job of type-casting. You are staging a celebration in the style and atmosphere of the last century. Some people would go even farther where I'm concerned and suggest that I belong to the Ice Age.

Speech, Columbia, Ga., 7/4/68

I bled easily in those days. My heart was filled with a great tenderness for all and sundry who came crying to me to help them fight their battle against this foe or that. Only finally I discovered that all too many of these organizations and the groups that they sponsored were as phoney as a three-dollar bill. They looked genuine enough but that was all.

Ronald Reagan; Governor & Statesman, 1968

CRITICISM CONCERNING HIS NOT BEING CONSERVA-
TIVE ENOUGH — I think there are some people – a few –
who would want me to jump off a cliff with the flag flying.

5/11/67

The result is that we're beginning to ignore the sacredness of
the individual. If we keep going in that direction there can be
one outcome: our surrender to a totally government planned
and controlled society. And when it happens it will be called
the "fulfillment of the liberal dream." But in fact it will be
fascism, because that's what fascism is: private ownership
with total government control.

Call to Action, 1976

...and Liberals

I was a near hopeless hemophilic liberal.

1947

The spectre our well-meaning liberal friends refuse to face is
that their policy of accommodation is appeasement, and
appeasement does not give you a choice between peace and
war, only between fight or surrender.

TV Adress, 10/27/64

My erstwhile associates in organized labor at the top level of
the AFL-CIO assail me as a "strident voice of the right wing
lunatic fringe." Sadly I have come to realize that a great many
so-called liberals aren't liberal – they will defend to the death
your right to agree with them.

Where's the Rest of Me?, 1965

Something the liberal will have to explain and stand trial for is his inability to see the Communist as he truly is and not as some kind of Peck's Bad Boy of liberalism who is basically all right but just a bit overboard and rough-edged. This ideological myopia is even true of some who have met the Reds in philosophical combat and who should have learned something from crossing swords.

Where's the Rest of Me?, 1965

Communists

I was truly so naive I thought the nearest Communists were fighting in Stalingrad.

Where's the Rest of Me?, 1965

The Communist plan for Hollywood was remarkably simple. It was merely to take over the motion picture business. Not only for its profit, as the hoodlums had tried – but also for a grand world-wide propaganda base.

Where's the Rest of Me?, 1965

My own test for the time when the Communists may call themselves a legitimate political party is that time when, in the USSR, an effective anti-Communist political party wins an election. At that time, I shall withdraw my objections to labeling Communists "political."

Where's the Rest of Me?, 1965

More than 2,000 years ago Demosthenes said to his fellow Athenians, "What sane man would let another man's words rather than his deeds determine whether he is at war or at peace with him?" The Russians can talk peace, but their actions belie their words.

Call to Action, 1976

I abhor the Communist philosophy, but I hope that we are never prompted by fear of communism into compromising our democratic principles.

Ronnie & Jesse, 1969

There are the outright Communists, of course, but many people are influenced who never realize it.

Ronnie & Jesse, 1969

Those who deplore use of the terms "pink" and "leftist" are themselves guilty of branding all who oppose their liberalism as right wing extremists. How long can we afford the luxury of this family fight when we are at war with the most dangerous enemy ever known to man?

TV Address, 10/27/64

HOUSE UNAMERICAN ACTIVITIES COMMITTEE —The hearings aroused the American people as they've never been aroused before or, sadly enough, since about Communism. Perhaps part of it was the thought of shelling out money at the box office to support some bum and his swimming pool while he plotted the country's destruction.

Where's the Rest of Me?, 1965

Law & Order

One way to make sure crime doesn't pay would be to let the Government run it.

Dallas, 10/26/67

As I learned, professional burglars seldom carry guns themselves, and would be overjoyed if no one else did either.

There is no single reason why the crime rate keeps rising in America. But up near the top of the list must be the sad fact that so much of our criminal justice system has become a technical game between lawyers, without regard for guilt or innocence.

Now the opponents of capital punishment in California and in the other states where it has been restored are asking why the rates of murder and other capital crimes haven't declined. In my opinion it's because there hasn't yet been an execution.

Call to Action, 1976

I once played a sheriff who thought he could do the job without a gun. I was dead in twenty-seven minutes of a thirty minute show.

Well, God help us if a burglar prowling the street at night has a government guarantee that there is no gun in any home he may choose to enter.

Call to Action, 1976

When I was governor, we invested heavily in probation programs. We felt, as everyone feels, that throwing youngsters into prison was like sending them to a school for crime. I'm afraid the juvenile delinquents were just as overjoyed at the chance to develop their criminal skills outside of prison.

Call to Action, 1976

It's obvious that prosperity doesn't decrease crime, just as it's obvious that deprivation and want don't necessarily increase crime. It's my recollection that crime rates were at their lowest during the Depression of the thirties, when great numbers of people were destitute. Today's criminals, for the most part, are not desperate people seeking bread for their families. Crime is the way they've chosen to live.

Call to Action, 1976

Our city streets are jungle paths after dark, with more crimes of violence than New York, Pennsylvania and Massachusetts combined.

1/4/66

I think that if we are going to ask men to engage in an occupation in which they protect us at the risk of their life, we of society have an obligation to them to let them know that society will do whatever it can to minimize the danger of their occupations. I think any policeman is entitled to that. There are no bands playing or flags flying when he shoots it out with a criminal on our behalf.

1966

Certainly, when no city street is safe for our women after dark, we have the right to insist that the victim of crime has rights at least equal to those of the criminal in protection under the law.

RACIAL DISTURBANCES — I think they have to be met and controlled, and whatever force is necessary to preserve law and order must be exerted.

Where's the Rest of Me?, 1965

For all our science and sophistication, for all our justified pride in intellectual accomplishment, the jungle is waiting to take over. The man with the badge helps to hold it back.

Position Paper, 1968

Civil Rights

Baseball is not only a symbol of competition without rancor, but also in recent years has offered Negroes of athletic ability unparalleled chances for *fame* and *success*. I am pleased that it is now time to play ball. The nation will be better off for it.

California Living Magazine, 12/31/67

Bigotry is something I feel so strongly about that I get a lump in my throat when I'm accused falsely!

It is the responsibility of the government, at point of bayonet if necessary, to see that every citizen gets their Constitutional individual rights and is not denied them by any group or individuals.

There is no law saying the Negro has to live in Harlem or Watts.

BLACKS — The Democratic Party is offering them one kind of paternalism for another. The Republican Party is offering them an individual destiny, the right to be free.

With the trouble going on today, and the bitter feelings engendered by extremists, both Negro and white, I can't help but point out my conviction that among the extremists you'll find no one who ever participated in athletics on a team that numbered among its personnel both Negroes and whites.

Where's the Rest of Me?, 1965

MILITANT BLACK LEADERS — You settle one thing with them and they will be back with another point. Some of them think they have found a pretty good thing.

Where's the Rest of Me?, 1965

MURDER OF MARTIN LUTHER KING — I hope that the major league baseball season opening tomorrow will mean a return to normalcy and turn our minds to the better side of our national life.

4/16/68

I just am incapable of prejudice; I believe this.

CESAR CHAVEZ — His terror tactics easily match those of the old-time night riders in the South. Incidentally, he's the only man I've ever known who can go on a fast and gain weight.

Letter to Gov. Robert Ray of Iowa

Years later in the dark depression years when he was trying to earn a buck on the road as a shoe salesman, he checked into a small town hotel. "Fine," said the clerk, reversing the register and reading his name. "You'll like it here, Mr. Reagan. We don't permit a Jew in the place." My father picked up his suitcase again. "I'm a Catholic," he said furiously, "and if it's come to the point where you won't take Jews, you won't take me either." Since it was the only hotel in town, he spent the night in his car in the snow. He contracted near-pneumonia and a short time later had the first heart attack of the several that led to his death.

Where's the Rest of Me?, 1965

It is very apparent in Detroit right now that these are no longer riots connected with civil rights in any way. These are riots of the lawbreakers and the mad dogs against the people.

1967

FATHER —He believed literally that all men were created equal and that man's own ambition determined what happened to him after that. He put his principles into practice. On the occasion when that early film classic, *The Birth of a Nation*, came to town, my brother and I were the only kids not to see it. "It deals with the Ku Klux Klan against the colored folks," Jack said sternly, "and I'm damned if anyone in this family will go see it.

Where's the Rest of Me?, 1965

49

Morality

WATERGATE — It was just a rude shock. It was a little bit like seeing civilization with its pants down to suddenly see a man sitting with his most intimate counselors and associates in a room obviously talking in ways that none of them would ever talk out in public.

San Francisco Chronicle, 6/1/74

"If it feels good, do it." "Whatever's right." But right for whom? "If it feels good, do it" is a good slogan until someone wants to feel good by hitting you over the head.

Call to Action, 1976

The traditional immorality of politics is no defense of Watergate. It's obvious, though, that the press wouldn't have been as interested in Watergate if the Democrats had been the culprits, which in itself is an indictment against the morality even of those who ferreted out the Watergate immorality. They weren't objectively ferreting out immorality; they were trying to prove that the faction they disagreed with had played "dirty tricks" on the faction they supported.

Call to Action, 1976

Nelle had raised us to believe the Lord's share was a tenth. I still believe it. Nelle could even put it on an almost selfish basis by guaranteeing that the Lord would make your 90 per cent twice as big if you made sure He got His tenth.

Where's the Rest of Me?, 1965

Somehow I've never had any trouble reconciling spiritual and scientific versions of creation. God's miracles are to be found in nature itself; the wind and waves, the wood that becomes a tree — all of these are explained biologically, but behind them is the hand of God. And I believe this is true of creation itself.

Sincerely, Ronald Reagan, 1967

You know, man in his entire history has adopted about 4 billion laws – and we haven't improved the Ten Commandments an iota.

Sincerely, Ronald Reagan, 1967

I am deeply concerned with the wave of hedonism – the humanist philosophy so prevalent today – and believe this nation must have a spiritual rebirth.

Sincerely, Ronald Reagan, 1967

Jack Webb has done some Dragnets on the subject of pornography, on drugs – things of this kind that I think should be educational features and used in schools.

How do you discuss sex in schools without discussing morality?

5/5/69

HIS STAFF — They work like hell. Sometimes I find them still working at nine o'clock at night. I don't like it. I try to send them home. I've told them we can't do it all in one day.

2/26/67

The biggest joke in Paris, France, is that instead of selling French postcards, they're selling California postcards.

Gubernatorial Campaign

We are told God is dead. Well, he isn't. We just can't talk to Him in the classroom anymore.

HOMOSEXUALS' PLACE — Well, maybe in the Department of Parks and Recreation.

Yale, 1967

The Pope has been most helpful to the United States in the international effort to reduce drug traffic. However, he was concerned whether this alone could solve the problem. I told him of my own feeling that it could not, that it was almost like carrying water in a sieve.

Letter to Reverend John J. McVernon, 1967

It fills me with terror to think of seminaries turning out class after class of clergymen who, apparently, are more social worker than minister, and to read of an entire denomination teaching young people to approach the Bible with their own beliefs as to what they should and should not accept.

Letter to Billy Graham, 1967

DREW PEARSON ALLEGES HOMOSEXUALITY AMONG REAGAN STAFF — Pearson had better not spit on the sidewalk if he returns to California.

Reagan: The Political Chameleon, 1976

If anything, I'm an ex-Democrat-Republican.

I don't think a candidate for president should dignify a pornographic magazine by giving interviews.

Denver, 10/28/76

DIVORCE — I suppose there had been warning signs, if only I hadn't been so busy, but small-town boys grow up thinking only other people get divorced.

SEXY FILMS — What writing does it take to simply have two people undress and get into bed?

TO THE MORAL MAJORITY — I know you can't endorse *me*.
I want you to know that I endorse *you.*

Newsweek, 9/15/80

Acting

THE BONZO FILM — The idea was to raise Bonzo in a home
exactly like a child, and see to what level environment could
lift his ability to learn. On the set he learned our business so
well that going to work was a fascinating experience.
Naturally his trainer was on the set, and the normal procedure
called for the director, Fred de Cordova, to tell the trainer
what we wanted from Bonzo. But time after time Freddie, like
the rest of us, was so captivated that he'd forget and start to
direct Bonzo as he did the human cast members. He'd say,
"No, Bonzo, in this scene you should. . . " Then he'd hit his
head and cry, "What the hell am I doing?"

Where's the Rest of Me?, 1965

ELECTED GOVERNOR — I don't know – I've never played a
governor before.

Sacramento Bee, 8/3/65

Suddenly now that I want to be something else besides an
actor – everybody is saying that I'm an actor. I'll probably be
the only fellow who will get an Oscar posthumously.

Orange County, California, 3/30/66

So much of our profession is taken up with pretending, with
the interpretation of never-never roles, that an actor must
spend at least half his waking hours in fantasy, in rehearsal or
shooting. If he is only an actor, I feel, he is much like I was in
King's Row, only half a man – no matter how great his talents.

Where's the Rest of Me?, 1965

I suppose, that I just liked showing off.

The Rise of Ronald Reagan, 1968

My heart is a hamloaf.

Where's the Rest of Me?, 1965

I didn't wear makeup in movies – there were some of us lucky enough to be able to get away with it.

4/1/74

FUND-RAISING — It's a chore to be done, and a fact of life is you're better box office the farther off from home you are.

Dallas, 10/26/67

TO GEORGE MURPHY, DANCER-TURNED-SENATOR —
George, here we are on the late show again.

Gubernatorial Inauguration, 1/3/67

Today, however, if I could give one bit of advice to youngsters starting out in theater or movies I'd say: don't marry your leading man or leading lady until you've done another role opposite someone else. Leadingladyitis is an infatuation that won't hold up, once the play is over and you each go back to playing yourselves.

Where's the Rest of Me?, 1965

I saw *Knute Rockne* one night, and it was so hacked up, my eighty-yard run was a five-yard loss.

Where's the Rest of Me?, 1965

I became the Errol Flynn of the B's. I was as brave as Errol, but in a low-budget fashion.

Where's the Rest of Me?, 1965

HIS DAUGHTER — She could marry both an actor and a politician without committing bigamy.

In show business we used to say that if you don't sing or dance, you wind up an after-dinner speaker.

Time, 11/26/79

...and Hollywood

I know the public has been fed a lot of drivel under the name of publicity, so we can understand their false ideas about us. But believe me, I have found this place to be pretty much a cross section of the U.S.A.

The Rise of Ronald Reagan, 1968

I did a string of pictures with the Dead End Kids, which was an experience similar to going over Niagara Falls in a barrel the hard way – upstream. Counting noses and getting them all in one scene was a major chore. You never knew when a canvas chair would go up in smoke, or be blown apart by the giant firecrackers they were never without. Having heard lurid tales from other actors, I approached my first picture with them in something of a sweat. Jimmy Cagney solved my problem one noon at the corner table. Having had his beginnings in the same New York Hell's Kitchen, he understood these kids as no one else could. "It's very simple," he said, "Just tell them you look forward to working with them but you'll slap hell out of them if they do one thing out of line." He was right – it was just that simple. I had the only unscorched chair on the set.

Where's the Rest of Me?, 1965

A lot of the crying sounds coming out of our studios today are like a guy sitting on a nail, too lazy to get up from what's hurting him.

Interview with Hedda Hopper, 1956

Everyone wants escape stuff.

PLAYING WESTERNS — I wanted action stuff.

ON THE SET — I moved in like there was no tomorrow, and the next thing the studio came undone like a wet cigar. I discovered that a kiss is only beautiful to the two people engaged in doing it. If you really kiss a girl, it shoves her face out of shape. I had to draw back and start over with the realization that work is work, and fun is fun.

Where's the Rest of Me?, 1965

In my previous career – motion pictures – we had a truism about people who 'went Hollywood' – they always were that way. Hollywood just exposed it.

Sincerely, Ronald Reagan, 1967

I don't care what they say about being avant garde or anything else. Frankly, call me square if you want to.

10/4/69

I do not believe the Communists have ever at any time been able to use the motion picture screen as a sounding board for their philosophy or ideology.

HUAC Testimony, 1947

Women

Not long ago I was interviewed by a woman who asked if my wife Nancy is liberated. I told her I wasn't sure what she meant. "Well," she said, "is Nancy just your wife or does she have a life of her own?" I told her that we think of ourselves as a team. Nancy doesn't need liberating because she doesn't think of herself as being my chattel in any way. She made up her own mind that marriage was a career in itself, and she does darned well at it.

Maybe the trouble with those professional "women's libbers" I mentioned earlier is related to something Will Rogers once said, "If women go on trying to be more and more equal to men, some day they won't know any more than men do."

Call to Action, 1976

We should never forget that women are the civilizing influence of our society. If it weren't for the influence of women, men would still be carrying clubs. You can easily observe the coarseness that comes over a group of men removed, for any reason, from the feminine influence.

Call to Action, 1976

Any man can find a twerp here and there who will go along with cheating and it doesn't take all that much manhood. It does take quite a man to remain attractive and be loved by a woman who has heard him snore, seen him unshaven, tended him while he was sick, and washed his dirty underwear. Do that and keep her still feeling a warm glow and you will know some very beautiful music.

Letter to son Michael

I think women should play a much larger role in government. I think they'd tend to be more realistic and candid, that they'd expect people to take care of themselves more. I think there would be fewer elaborate systems for government interference.

... and Youth

They're what this election is all about. I'd like them to know the freedom we knew when we were their age.

Time, 10/20/80

TO BRITISH EXPORTERS — I was surprised you hadn't retaliated for some of the movies we sent you. But lately I've been listening to some of the records bought by my children and I think you're beginning to get even.

All kids are sentimental.

But I do know that we've swallowed what I'd call the "Dr. Spock syndrome," wherein we question our own values and whether we have a right to impose our beliefs on our children. And in doing so, we've weakened the family.

Call to Action, 1976

A child in America should grow up with the assurance that his parents have accepted the responsibility for defining right and wrong.

Call to Action, 1976

There is a growing tendency for schools and even some churches to challenge the mores and values of parents, to encourage a young person to develop his own ideas and standards. That's healthy only if the young person already has the maturity of having accepted and lived with a set of values in his own family. Otherwise he is likely to fall victim to the first doctrinaire teacher or minister who gets to him, just to maintain a sense of security. That's when education becomes indoctrination.

Call to Action, 1976

They have found a substance in marijuana which is very close to the female hormone. Some men find they are developing feminine characteristics.

Congressional Quarterly, 1976

I don't think it's necessary to win a popularity contest with your kids, and especially not while they're kids. Parents should be more concerned with what their kids will think of them when they reach thirty. Or, more importantly, what their kids will think of themselves. Most of us, when we look back over our lives and our reactions to our parents, discover that today we accept and are grateful for things we rebelled against at the age of fifteen or twenty.

Call to Action, 1976

In New York recently at a dinner party a prominent editor sought the advice of several of us on 'What do you tell a teen-ager who uses pot?' I said, 'Why don't you tell him if you catch him with one of those things in his mouth you'll kick his bottom side up between his shoulders?'

Sincerely, Ronald Reagan, 1967

I don't feel that a family should cling to its young to the point that they're reluctant ever to leave the nest. Quite the contrary. I think the whole duty of parents is to bring their children up with a sense of values to the point where, with confidence, they can throw them out of the nest and start them on their way.

Call to Action, 1976

The Friend

NIXON'S PHLEBITIS — Maybe that will satisfy the lynch mob.

Congressional Quarterly, 1976

The American

JOHN WAYNE — He gave the whole world an image of what an American should be.

Reader's Digest, 1979

Observe the Rules or Get Out.

Plaque Above Entrance to Gov. Reagan's Office, 1966